Alchemy
Reference Guide

A Tool for Exploring the Secret Art
by Dennis William Hauck

CONTENTS

Athanor Books

Athanor Books
AlchemyStudy.com
ISBN 0-9637914-6-X

ALCHEMY DICTIONARY

- A -

Ablation is the Separation of a component of a substance by removing the upper part; skimming off the surface of a compound; separating a component by whisking the surface with a feather or cloth.

Ablution is the washing of a solid with a liquid, usually in plain water. Generally, it is purification by successive washings in a liquid. Spiritually and psychologically, it is facing one's emotions and letting feelings flow, so that innocence and purity can be restored. Baptism.

Abstraction is a process of sublimation or distillation.

Aes Cyprium is Cyprian brass or copper.

Aion (see Ouroboros)

Air is one of the Four Elements of alchemy. Air in the alchemical sense carries the archetypal properties of spirit into the manifested world. It is associated with the operation of Separation and represented by the metal Iron.

Albification is making the matter in the alchemical work become white. Refers to both physical and spiritual processes.

Alchemy The word is derived from the Arabian phrase "al-khemia," which refers to the preparation of the Stone or Elixir by the Egyptians. The Arabic root "khemia" comes from the Coptic "khem" that alluded to the fertile black soil of the Nile delta. Esoterically and hieroglyphically, the

word refers to the dark mystery of the primordial or First Matter (the Khem), the One Thing through which all creation manifests. Alchemy, then, is the Great Work of nature that perfects this chaotic matter, whether it is expressed as the metals, the cosmos, or the substance of our souls.

Alembic is the upper part of a still; a stillhead, a type of retort. The term is often used to refer to a complete still. (see cucurbit; Distillation)

Alkahest is the power from Above that makes possible alchemical transformation. The word is usually translated as "universal solvent," which alludes to the ability of the alkahest to dissolve or reduce all physical matter to its basic essence. With metals, this meant transmuting them to their purest form, which was gold. In the human body, this meant the creation or revealing of a golden body of consciousness, the Astral Body.

Aludel is a pear-shaped earthenware bottle, open at both ends. It was used as a condenser in the sublimation process and thus came to signify the end-stages of transformation. Also called the Hermetic Vase, the Philosopher's Egg, and the Vase of the Philosophy.

Amalgamation is the formation of an amalgam, or alloy, of a metal with mercury. This term is sometimes extended to mean any union of metals. Amalgam.

Angel An angel in alchemical treatises symbolizes sublimation or the ascension of the volatile principle.

Animals are often used to symbolize the basic components and processes of alchemy. They may be used to symbolize the four Elements such as the lion or ox (Earth), fish or whales (Water), eagles (Air), or salamanders or dragons (Fire). Aerial animals generally indicate volatile principles, while terrestrial animals indicate fixed principles. Whenever two animals are found, they signify Sulfur and Mercury or some relationship between the fixed and the volatile.

Ankh is a hieroglyphic character used by Egyptian alchemists to denote the ascendancy of the life force or spirit (the circle) over the material world (the cross). In other words, through crucifixion, the soul rises and is reborn on a higher level. Its use dates back over 3,000 years and is a symbolic rendition of the principles expressed in the Emerald Tablet. In its design, the circular One Mind projects downward into the One Thing, while the lateral manifested world on which we are crucified is indicated by the horizontal bar.

Antimony is from the Latin word "antimonium" used by Constantinius Africanus (1050 AD) to refer to stibnite ore. The metal antimony symbolizes the animal nature or wild spirit of man and nature, and it was often symbolized by the wolf. Alchemist Basil Valentine named the metal, after feeding it to some monks in a Benedictine monastery. The monks got violently ill and some even died, hence the Latin name that means "anti-monk." Spiritually too, monks feel most threatened by their own animal nature. Oddly enough, the Tincture of Antimony cures venereal diseases. Associated with the attributes of Lead.

Apollo References to the Greek god Apollo signify the Sun as spirit or solar consciousness.

Aqua fortis is Latin for "strong water" and refers to nitric acid. Various grades of *aqua fortis* were prepared depending on the length of its Distillation, which concentrated the acid. A mixture of *aqua fortis* and *spiritus salis* ("spirit of salt," i.e., hydrochloric acid) produces *aqua regia* ("royal water" -- so named because it can dissolve gold). It was first prepared by distilling common salt with *aqua fortis*.

Aqua tofani is the oxide of arsenic. It was extremely poisonous but used by Paracelsus medicinally.

Aqua vitae is "living water" or water "with spirit." An aqueous alcohol concentrated by one or more Distillations.

Arcana ("magical secrets") are archetypal influences that transcend space and time. According to the ancient text *Archidoxies*, the arcana are pre-existing powers that "have the power of transmuting, altering, and restoring us." In this view, the arcana are the secret workings of the mind of God, the *logos* of the Greeks or what the alchemists referred to as the thoughts of the One Mind. In the Tarot, the arcana are represented by symbolic drawings that the reader tries to work with through meditation. In the Cabala, the arcana are represented by the esoteric properties of the letters of the Hebrew alphabet, energies that the cabalist tries to work with in the Tree of Life. In the in the ancient Chinese system of divination, the *I Ching*, the arcana are represented by the sixty-four trigrams, each with its own properties and influences. The alchemists believed the arcana were expressed on all levels of reality -- from chemical compounds to our innermost moods and desires.

Arcanum Experiment The early alchemists divided their chemicals into major and minor arcana. The major arcana consisted of the four compounds: Vitriol, Natron, Liquor Hepatis, and Pulvis Solaris. Three out of the four consisted of dual ingredients that were easily separable. Vitriol could be broken down into sulfuric acid and iron. Natron appeared as sodium carbonate and sodium nitrate. Pulvis Solaris was made up of the red and black varieties. Thus, the seven chemicals comprising the minor arcana were: Sulfuric Acid, Iron, Sodium Carbonate, Sodium Nitrate, Liquor Hepatis, Red Pulvis Solaris, and Black Pulvis Solaris. The alchemists believed that these secret chemicals could be combined in the Arcanum Experiment, the single laboratory experiment that would demonstrate the archetypal forces and evolution of the universe. Ideally, such an experiment should succeed on many levels, not only corroborating the deepest philosophical and psychological principles, but also providing concrete evidence of their veracity. The Arcanum Experiment exposed the hidden principles connecting heaven and earth, offering a framework in which to explain both microcosmic and macrocosmic events.

Archaeus is the "Thing Itself" of a substance. According to Paracelsus, it is the "secret inner matter of a substance," its oldest part that goes back to when it was just an ideal image, thought, or vibration of spirit in the Above.

Archetype is an elementary idea rooted in the mind. It is the ideal or essence from which an existing thing has been copied and is part of creation itself. Archetypes are primordial patterns that show up on all levels of reality.

Ascension occurs when the active or subtle part of a solution rises up in the flask, usually by heating.

Assation is the reduction of a substance to a dry ash by roasting.

Athanor comes from the Arabic word "al-tannur" (oven), the athanor is the furnace used by the alchemists to perfect matter. Built of brick or clay, the athanor usually was shaped like a tower with a domed roof and was designed to keep an even heat over long periods of time. The alchemists considered it an incubator and sometimes referred to it as the "House of the Chick." Symbolically, the athanor is also the human body and the fire of bodily metabolism that fuels our transformation and the ultimate creation of a Second Body of light. The mountain is a symbol for the athanor, since the perfection of the metals takes place under the guise of Nature within mountains. Sometimes a hollow oak tree is used to symbolize the athanor.

Azoth. The term "Azoth" is formed from the first and last letters of the English alphabet ("a" and "z"), which stand for the beginning and end of all creation -- the alpha and omega of the Greek philosophers, the aleph and tau of the Hebrew cabalists. Therefore the Azoth is the ultimate arcanum, the universal spirit of God in all created things. The alchemists believed that the liquid metal mercury carried the signature of this omnipotent archetypal spirit.

- B -

Bain Marie (Balneum Marie) is a warm alchemical bath. Chemically, it is a double-boiler in which a container of water is suspended in a simmering cauldron. Psychologically, it is the gentle warmth of emotionally centered meditation used in the Dissolution process. The Bain Marie was named after Maria Prophetissa, a Jewish alchemist who wrote much about the methods and equipment of the Water operations of Dissolution and Distillation.

Balsam is a resinous or waxy semi-solid compound that captures the essence of a liquid medicine or perfume. To Paracelsus, the balsam was the "interior salt" that protected the body from decomposition, and earlier alchemists considered the Balsam of the Elements to be the Quintessence, the result of the Conjunction of alchemical principles. Because of it amalgamating ability, mercury was considered the balsam agent of the metals. In the chemical arcana, Liquor Hepatis mixed with fat or wax was known as the Balsam of the Soul.

Basilisk is a symbolic alchemical creature said to have the head of a bird and the body of a dragon. The wingless serpentine animal was hatched from a hermaphroditic cock's egg and nursed by a serpent. Psychologically, the Basilisk represents the melding of our higher and lower natures in Conjunction, a process that must be continued in the next three operations of alchemy for this "Child of the Philosophers" to become the Living Stone of the fully integrated Self. Biologically, the Basilisk represents the mammalian embryology, the genetic replaying of the stages of evolution within the egg or womb. The Basilisk also has chemical connotations, which probably have to do with a metallurgical process involving cinnabar.

Baths in alchemy symbolize the Dissolution process in which the metals are cleansed and purified.

Bezoar. Some chemical compounds, such as sulfur auretum when mixed with either red mercuric oxide or black antimony, clump together inseparably as soon as they are mixed together. The alchemists considered such compounds to be chemical bezoars, which are hard clumps of undigested food or solid balls of hair sometimes found in the intestines. In the Middle Ages, physicians thought the strange mass protected people from poisons and actually prescribed it to their patients. Egyptian priests discovered bezoars during the preparation of mummies and believed the hard balls were magical pills formed by the large serpent in man (the intestines). Some evidence suggests that the Egyptians also looked for a similar pill in the small serpent in man (the brain) and found it there in the form of the pineal gland. This pine-shaped gland is imbedded with tiny crystals of dark melanin, and could explain the Egyptian pinecone emblems and the origin of the caduceus itself. And, in the same way that bezoars were formed in the serpentine contours of the intestines, so was gold formed in the bowels of the earth: gold was considered a mineral bezoar.

Birds Ascending birds indicate the volatilization of compounds or their sublimation. Descending birds indicate the fixation of compounds or their condensation and precipitation. Birds shown both ascending and descending indicate the process of Distillation.

Bismuth is a hard and brittle metallic element whose ore is grayish-white with a tinge of red. The crystals are octahedrons and often found in nature with cobalt deposits. It is used to make alloys of low melting point.

Black Lion is the darkest part of a substance, its *caput mortum* or black salt that cannot be purified any more. Carbon.

Black Phase (or Melanosis) is the first stage in alchemy. It phase begins with the operation of Calcination and lasts through the Putrefaction stage of Fermentation.

Blue Vitriol (see Bluestone)

Bluestone is cupric sulfate.

Brimstone (from German "brennstein" or "burning stone"). Sulfur.

Butter of Antimony is white crystal-line antimony trichloride. Made by Basil Valentine by distilling roasted stibnite with corrosive sublimate. Glauber later prepared it by dis-solving stibnite in hot concentrated hydrochloric acid and distilling the solution.

Butter of Tin is hydrated stannic chloride.

- C -

Cadmia (Tuttia or Tutty) is zinc carbonate.

Caduceus is the magical staff of Hermes, the Messenger of the Gods and revealer of alchemy. The staff is entwined by two serpents representing the solar and lunar forces. Their union is the Conjunction of alchemical principles and their offspring, if it lives, is the Stone. This Stone is represented as a golden ball with wings at the top of the caduceus.

Calamine is another word for zinc carbonate.

Calcination is the first operation in alchemical transformation. It is denoted by the symbol for the first sign of the zodiac, Aries. Breaking down of a substance by fierce heating and burning usually in an open crucible.

Calomel is mercurous chloride. It is a purgative, made by subliming a mixture of mercuric chloride and metallic mercury, triturated in a mortar. This was heated in an iron pot and the crust of calomel formed on the lid was ground to powder and boiled with water to remove the very poisonous mercuric chloride.

Cassel Yellow (see Naples Yellow)

Caustic Marine Alkali is caustic soda. Sodium hydroxide. Made by adding lime to Natron.

Caustic Soda is sodium hydroxide.

Caustic Volatile Alkali is ammonium hydroxide.

Caustic Wood Alkali is caustic potash. Potassium hydroxide. Made by adding lime to potash.

Cementation is acting upon a substance by mixing it in layers with a powdered (often corrosive) material, such as lime. This mixture is then be made to react and weld together by heating to a high temperature in a cementing furnace.

Ceration is a part of the Fermentation process during which a waxy substance flows from the putrefied matter. This is the Ferment, the precursor of the Stone. Ceration is the softening or mollification of a hard material to change it into a more waxy state; covering with wax or salve. Making of a substance to soften and appear like wax was often accomplished by continually adding a liquid and heating.

Chalk is calcium carbonate.
Child A naked child symbolizes the innocent soul. In alchemy, the child is the offspring of the King and Queen, the result of their marriage or union. A child crowned or clothed in purple robes signifies Salt or the Philosopher's Stone.

Chrome Green is chromic oxide.

Chrome Orange is a mixture of chrome yellow and chrome red.

Chrome Red is basic lead chromate.

Chrome Yellow is lead chromate.

Cibation is the addition of new material to the contents of the crucible. During Dissolution, it requires adding liquid to the desiccated matter at precisely the right moment.

Cineration (incineration) is the reduction of a substance to ashes by heating.

Cinnabar (Vermillion) is the bright red ore of mercury sulfide. Known as "Dragon's Blood," the roasted rocks emit a thick reddish smoke, as pure glistening mercury oozes from cracks. Psychologically, cinnabar represents the hardened habits and terrestrial marriages of soul and spirit that must be broken asunder in Calcination to free the essences with which the alchemist intends to work.

Circle or sphere is symbolic of unity, the One Mind of god. It is mathematically and psychologically an "irrational" experience beyond the duality of reason.

Circulation is the purification of a substance by a circular distillation in a pelican or closed distillation apparatus. Through heating the liquid component separates, is condensed and descends again to the substance in the flask. Sometimes it refers to a rotation, in which a liquid is circulated over a solid in a sealed vessel.

Coadunation is another term for Coagulation.

Coagulation is the thickening of a thin liquid into a more solid mixture through some inner change, as with the curdling of milk. This can be accomplished by a variety of means - by the addition of a substance, by heating or cooling. Coagulation is the seventh and last operation in alchemical transformation is Coagulation.

Cobalt is named by the copper miners of the Hartz Mountains after the evil spirits the "kobolds" that gave a false copper ore.

Coction is the cooking or heating of a substance at a moderate heat for an extended period.

Cohobation is a kind of Distillation in which the distillate is poured back into its residue; a method of redistillation. Cohobation involves the frequent removal of the moist component of a substance by heating. Often the moist component (or some other liquid) is added and the process continued.

Colcothar is a red variety of ferric oxide formed by burning green vitriol in air.

Coliquation is the Conjunction or melting together of two fusible substances.

Coloration is tingeing a substance by adding a dye or colored tincture. Coloring can by either by tingeing the whole body or by producing a surface coating.

Combustion is the burning of a substance in the open air.

Comminution is the reduction of a substance into a powder, either by grinding, pulverizing, or forcing it through a sieve.

Composition is the joining together of two different substances.

Conception is the marriage or union of the male and female aspects of substances.

Concoction is the cooking or heating of a mixture of substances at a moderate heat for an extended period.

Condenser is a double-jacketed tube with water flowing though it to condense vapors into liquids.

Congelation is a loose or temporary Conjunction of opposites; a mixture in which a liquid is gelled or made semi-solid; intercourse. The process is represented by the sign for the constellation of Taurus. The conversion of a thin, easily flowing liquid into a congealed thick substance, often by heating.

Conglutination is the conversion of a substance into a gluey mass, often by a Putrefaction.

Conjunction is the fourth operation in alchemical transformation. It is the coming together of the opposing archetypal forces of the Sun and Moon or the King and Queen. Conjunction is the joining of two opposite components, often seen as the union of the male and female, the subtle and gross, or even the elements.

Contrition is the reduction of a substance into powder only by means of fire.

Copper Glance is cuprous sulfide ore.

Copper is one of the seven metals of alchemy. Copper (and sometimes bronze and brass) is associated with the operation of Conjunction and the element Earth.

Copulation is a Conjunction, or joining of two opposite components, seen through the metaphor of the union of the male and female, or the union of the fixed and the volatile.

Corrosion is the eating up of a substance by an acid, alkali or corrosive material.

Corrosive Sublimate is mercuric chloride. First mentioned by Geber, who prepared it by subliming mercury, calcined green vitriol, common salt and nitre.

Cribation is the reduction of a substance to a powder by forcing through a sieve or mesh.

Crosslet (see crucible)

Crown symbolizes the successful completion of an alchemical operation or the achievement of a magisterium. It also signifies chemical royalty or the perfection of a metal.

Crows are the symbols of the black phases of Calcination and Putrefaction.

Crucible is the melting vessel of the alchemists. It is made of inert material such as porcelain and can withstand great heat. Used to liquefy the metals.

Crystallization is the formation of crystals out of a solution of the substance usually in water, either by their gradual formation from the liquid, or by evaporation of the liquid.

Cupel is a small cup or dish made of bone-ash or other porous and infusible material. Cupellation is the process of heating a substance in a cupel in a current of air, such as done in the refining of silver and gold.
Cuprite is red cuprous oxide ore.

Cucurbit is the lower part of a still, containing the original liquid. It is made of glass or earthenware and was also known as a "gourd" on account of its shape; a receiver. (see alembic; Distillation)

- D -

Dealbation is the making of the black substance of the alchemical process become brilliant white.

Decoction is the digestion of a substance in the flask without the addition of any other material.

Decrepitation is the crackling and splitting apart of substances, for example common salt, on heating.

Deliquium is the reduction of a solid placed in a damp place to a liquid by its absorbing water from the air.

Descension is when the subtle or active part of a substance is made to go down to the bottom of a flask, rather than ascend as a vapor.

Desiccation is the drying or removal of all the moisture in a substance.

Detonation is the explosive burning of substances on heating, for example substances mixed with nitre.

Dew is symbolic of divine incarnation or manifestation from Above. Alchemists believed natural dew contained the divine Salt (thoughts of the One Mind) that could transform the Sulfur and Mercury of the First Matter. In many ways, dew represented the Elixir or contents of the cup of God, the Holy Grail.

Diana Appearances of the Greek goddess Diana in alchemical drawings and treatises signify the Moon and Lunar consciousness.

Digestion is a kind of Putrefaction in which the nutrients or essences are reabsorbed; the slow modification of a substance by means of a gentle heat.

Disintegration is the breaking down or dissociation of a substance into different parts.

Dispoliaration is the dissolving or transforming of a dead substance into a liquid.

Dissociation is the breaking down or disintegration of a substance into different parts.

Dissolution is the second operation in alchemical transformation. The process of dissolving a solid in a liquid; the reduction of a dry thing in water. Represented by the sign for the constellation of Cancer. The dissolving or transforming of a substance into a liquid.

Distillation is the sixth operation in alchemical transformation. Denoted by the symbol for the constellation Virgo. It is essentially a process of concentration, no matter on what level (physical, mental, or spiritual) it occurs. The separation of a volatile component from a substance by heating so as to drive off the component as a vapor that is condensed and collected in a cooler part of the apparatus. The entire setup consisting of the boiling flask, condensing tube, and receiving flask is called a Distillation Train.

Divaporation is an exhalation of dry vapors from a substance, which can occur at different degrees of heat.

Division is the separation of a substance into its elements.

Dogs signify primitive matter, natural sulfur, or material gold. A dog being devoured by a wolf symbolizes the process of purifying gold using antimony.

Dove is a symbol of renewed spirit or infusion of energy from Above. Chemically, it signifies the change from the Black Stage to the White Phase of transformation.

Dragon in flames is a symbol of fire and Calcination. Several dragons fighting is symbolic of Putrefaction. Dragons with wings represent the volatile principle; dragons without wings represent the fixed principle. A dragon biting its own tale is the Ouroboros and signifies the fundamental unity of all things. In formulae, the term "the Dragon" usually refers to the mercury-acid obtained from metals. When winged, it is volatile (spiritual or pure); without wings, it is fixed (crude or material).

Dulcify means to sweeten.

Dutch White is mixture of one part of white lead to three of barium sulfate.

- E -

Eagle is always a symbol of volatilization. For instance, an eagle devouring a lion indicates the volatilization of a fixed component by a volatile component. Denotes sublimation or distillation.

Earth is one of the Four Elements of alchemy. Earth in the alchemical sense carries the archetypal properties of manifestation, birth, and material creation. It is associated with the operation of Conjunction and represented by the green ore of copper.

Ebullition is an effervescence produced through Fermentation.

Edulceration is the washing of a salty substance till all the salts are removed.

Egg is symbolic of the hermetically sealed vessel of creation. Stoppered retorts, coffins, and sepulchers represent eggs in many alchemical drawings.

Elaboration is the general term for the process of separating the pure from the impure, and leading a substance towards perfection, which can be done through a variety of means and processes.

Elevation is the raising of the subtle parts of a substance upwards, away from the bodily residues, into the upper parts of the vessel.

Elixeration is the conversion of a substance into an elixir.

Elixir of the alchemists is essentially a liquid version of the Philosopher's Stone and has the same ability to perfect any substance. When applied to the human body, the Elixir cures diseases and restores youth.

Evaporation is the removal of the watery part of a substance by gentle heating, or being left a long time in a dry place.

Exaltation is an operation by which a substance is raised into a purer and more perfect nature. Exaltation usually involves the release of a gas or air from a substance.

Expression is the extraction of juices by means of a press.

Extraction is the preparation of the subtler and purer parts of a substance, usually by macerating it in alcohol. The extract can then be separated from the residue.

- F -

Fermentation is the fifth operation in alchemical transformation. It is represented by the sign for the constellation of Capricorn. After the rotting of a substance, usually of an organic nature, digesting bacteria appear often accompanied by the release of gas bubbles.

Filtration is a kind of Separation, in which material is passed through a sieve or screen designed to allow only pieces of a certain size to pass through. The operation is represented by the sign for the constellation of Sagittarius, the Archer. The process or removing the grosser parts of a substance by passing through a strainer, filter or cloth.

Fire is one of the Four Elements of alchemy. Fire in the alchemical sense carries the archetypal properties of activity and transformation. It is associated with the operation of Calcination and represented by the metal lead.

Fire Stone is a transmuting Stone made from antimony.

Fixation is the make a volatile subject fixed, stable, or solid, so that it remains permanently unaffected by fire. The process of stabilizing and incarnating a substance; depriving a substance of its volatility or mobility to congeal or combine it. The process is represented by the sign for the constellation of Gemini.

Flores is the oxide of a metal.

Flowers of Sulfur are light yellow crystalline powder, made by distilling sulfur.

Foliation is the making some substances puff up in layers, like leaves laying on top of one another, usually undertaken by heating.

Fountain The alchemical Fountain of Fountains is a symbol of the Ouroboros. Three fountains represent the three principles of Sulfur, Mercury, and Salt. The King and Queen sitting in a fountain signifies a bath or the Water operations of Dissolution and Distillation.

Fulmination is the preparation of a fulminate or explosively unstable form of a metal. Sometimes applied to any process in which a sudden eruptive event occurs.

Fulminating Gold is made by adding ammonia to the auric hydroxide formed by precipitation by potash from metallic gold dissolved in aqua regis. Highly explosive when dry.

Fulminating Silver is silver nitride, very explosive when dry. Made by dissolving silver oxide in ammonia.

Fumigation is the alteration of a substance by exposing it to a corroding smoke.
Fusion is the joining of powdered substances together, or the conversion of a substance into a new form, by means of an extremely high degree of heat, sometimes using a flux.

- G -

Galena is plumbic sulfide, which is the chief ore of lead.

Geber is the Latin name of Jabir ibn Hayyan (721 - 815 A.D.). He is the father of both Islamic and European alchemy. He knew of the existence of the Emerald Tablet and spread the doctrines of the Four Elements and the Mercury-Sulfur theory of the generation of the metals.

Glass of Antimony is impure antimony tetroxide, obtained by roasting stibnite. Used as a yellow pigment for glass and porcelain.

Glauber's Salt is sodium sulfate.

Glutination is turning a substance into a gluey, glutinous mass.

Gold is the most perfect of the metals. For the alchemist, it repre-sented the perfection of all matter on any level, including that of the mind, spirit, and soul. It is associated with the final operation of Coagulation.

Gradation is the gradual purification of a substance, often through a series of stages.
Grain, seeds, or grapes symbolize the matter of the Stone, which is the life force itself.

Granulation is the reduction of a substance to grains or powder. There are various means of doing this - pounding, grinding, using thermal shock by heating and rapid cooling, and many others.

Green Dragon is probably an acetate of lead which originates from a green oil. Philosophically, the Green Dragon is a "tamed" dragon sharing the crystallized energy that it had formerly so ferociously protected. Psychologically, it represents elements of the unconscious that have been assimilated into consciousness.

Green Lion is the green acetate of lead in its liquid or crystallized form.

Green Vitriol is ferrous sulfate.

Griffin's Egg The griffin is a half-lion and half-eagle creature that symbolizes the Conjunction of the fixed and volatile principles. The Griffin Egg is an allusion to the Vessel of Hermes.

Grinding is the reduction of substances to a powder, usually through the use of a mortar and pestle.

Gypsum is calcium sulfate.

- H -

Hartshorn is a powder of crushed bone, horn, or nails. (see Sal Volatile).

Head is the top of a retort flask used in distillation. Sometimes it also refers to the spout/condenser of the classical retort.

Hermaphrodite represents Sulfur and Mercury after their Conjunction. *Rebis* (something double in characteristics) is another designation for this point in the alchemy of transformation.

Hermetically Sealed means sealed airtight so no outside influences might corrupt the contents.

Horn Silver is *Argentum cornu*, a glasslike ore of silver chloride.

Humectation is a process by which humidity is given to the substance, usually not by the direct addition of liquid, but by a gradual process of absorbing moisture.

- I -

Ignition is the self-calcination of a substance by it burning itself in a crucible.

Imbibition is the feeding of a process by the gradual and continuing addition of some substance. To imbibe means to pour a liquid onto a solid so that the solid (usually a salt) completely absorbs the liquid.

Impastation is when the matter undergoing putrefaction thickens or congeals into the consistency of molten black pitch.

Impregnation is the alchemical process is sometimes paralleled with the gestation of a child. Thus impregnation follows from the union or copulation of the male and female, and leads to the generation of a new substance.

Inceration (see Ceration) is the making of a substance into a soft waxy consistency, usually by combining it with water.

Incineration is the conversion of a substance to ashes by means of a powerful fire.

Incorporation is the mingling of mixed bodies into a conglomerate mass.

Ingression occurs when substances combine in such a manner that they cannot afterwards be separated.

Inhumation is to bury under the earth, sometimes used to mean any process that buries the active substance in a dark earthy material. Also applied to placing a flask in the warm heat of a dung bath.

Iosis (see Purple Phase)

Iron is one of the seven metals of alchemy. It is associated with the operation of Separation.

- J -

Jabir (see Geber)

Jungian Alchemy Psychiatrist Carl Gustav Jung rediscovered the images and principles of alchemy surfacing in the dreams and compulsions of his patients and began a lifelong study of the subject. He concluded that alchemical images explain the archetypal roots of the modern mind and underscores a process of transformation leading to the integration of the personality.

- K -

Kerckringus Menstruum is used to extract metallic oils. It is made from ethyl alcohol that has been distilled off an oil of thrice sublimated Hartsthorn (see Hartsthorn).

Kermes is the oil of antimony is its crude state. The reddish-brown liquid settles out of an alkaline menstruum by neutralization by an acid. In general, the term applies to any metallic oil that precipitates out of lye or other alkaline solution by neutralization.

King in alchemy represents man, solar consciousness, or Sulfur. The King is naked in the early operations of alchemy and regains his royal robes at the end of his transformation. The King united with the Queen symbolizes Conjunction.

King's Yellow is a mixture of orpiment with white arsenic.

- L -

Lapis Infernalis is silver nitrate.

Leach means to separate out pure salts from their mixture with pure salts by the dissolving the entire mixture in water and extracting the pure salts by filtration and evaporation.

Lead is the first and oldest of the seven metals of alchemy. It is associated with the operation of Calcination.

Lead Fume is a lead oxide obtained from the flues at lead smelters.

Lembic (see Alembic)

Leukosis (see White Phase)

Limatura Martis is iron filings.

Lion is any salt or fixed substance obtained from metals. It is red, green, or black according to its state of perfection.

Liquefaction is the turning of a solid material into a liquid, either by melting or dissolving.

Liquor Hepatis was the name given to a sulfurous liquid used by the alchemists. Considered the arcanum of the soul, Liquor Hepatis was prepared by distilling a solution of sulfur, lime, and sal ammoniac. The early alchemists secured lime (calcium oxide) by heating limestone and made sal ammoniac (ammonium chloride) by gently heating camel dung in sealed containers. The distillation for Liquor Hepatis produced a combination of hydrogen sulfide and ammonia gases. Since no solids precipitated, alchemists considered this an ascending reaction only. That was a significant fact to the Egyptians, who associated the Liquor with the soul. They believed the soul resided in the liver, and the reddish-brown color of Liquor Hepatis convinced them they had isolated the soul's essence. The name comes from "hepar," the Greek word for liver. The Liquor exuded an unnatural, pungent odor that the alchemists found quite mysterious. They assumed it was due to an ethereal presence concealed in the sulfur and activated by the fertile principle in ammonia. To the Egyptians, the odor symbolized a soul or a spiritized presence hidden within the liquid. They solidified that presence by adding wax and fat to Liquor Hepatis and turning it into a thick paste. The emulsion became known as the Balsam of the Alchemists or Balsam of the Soul. The possibility of coagulating an invisible potential into a second body, like a balsam, became a basic tenet of alchemy.

Litharge (or letharge) is the left-over scum, spume, or ashes of a metallic operation; reddish-yellow crystalline form of lead monoxide, formed by fusing and powdering massicot.

Liver of Sulfur is a complex of polysulfides of potassium, made by fusing potash and sulfur.

Lixiviation is the oxidation of sulfide ores by exposing them to air and water. This forms Vitriol.

Lunar Caustic (see *Lapis Infernalis*)

Luna Cornea is the soft colorless tough mass of silver chloride, made by heating horn silver till it forms a dark yellow liquid and then cooling. Described by Oswald Croll in 1608.

Luting is the sealing of a flask or other apparatus through the use of a lute, or resinous paste which once applied sets hard and produces an airtight seal.

- M -

Maceration is to soak a substance in a liquid to separate its components. Similar to chewing food and predigesting it with saliva.

Magnesia was a mystical term to the alchemists that denoted the primordial transforming substance in the universe. It was one of many symbols used to describe the central mystery of alchemy that was never to be spoken of in common wording.

Marcasite is the mineral form of Iron disulfide. Oxidizes in moist air to green vitriol.

Massicot is the yellow powder form of lead monoxide.

Matrass is a round-bottomed flask with a very long neck. Also called a "bolt-head."

Maturation is a general term applied to identify the appearance of a degree of perfection in the work.

Melanosis (see Black Phase)

Melting is the reduction of a metal or substance to a liquid through heating.

Menstruum is an alchemical term meaning a solvent or alkahest having both the power to dissolve and coagulate at the same time. Based on the belief that the ovum takes its life and form from the menses, the menstruum was also referred to the as the Mercury of the Philosophers.

Mercurius Praecipitatus is the red mercuric oxide described by Geber. Sometimes it refers to any amalgam of mercury.

Mercury, called quicksilver by the ancients, is a liquid metal that could be found weeping through cracks in certain rocks or accumulating in small puddles in mountain grottos. It was also obtained by roasting cinnabar (mercury sulfide). The shiny metal would seep from the rocks and drip down into the ashes, from which it was later collected. The early alchemists made red mercuric oxide by heating quicksilver in a solution of nitric acid. The acid, which later alchemists called "aqua fortis," was made by pouring sulfuric acid over saltpeter. The reaction of quicksilver in nitric acid is impressive. A thick red vapor hovers over the surface and bright red crystals precipitate to the bottom. This striking chemical reaction demonstrated the simultaneous separation of mercury into the Above and the Below. Mercury's all-encompassing properties were exhibited in other compounds too. If mercury was heated in a long-necked flask, it oxidized into a highly poisonous white powder (white mercuric oxide) and therapeutic red crystals (red mercuric oxide). Calomel (mercury chloride) was a powerful medicine, unless it was directly exposed to light, in which case it became a deadly poison. When mixed with other metals, liquid mercury tended to unite with them and form hardened amalgams. These and other properties convinced alchemists that mercury transcended both the solid and liquid states, both earth and heaven, both life and death. It symbolized Hermes himself, the guide to the Above and Below.

Milk of Sulfur (or *Lac Sulfuris*) is white colloidal sulfur. Geber made this by adding an acid to *thion hudor*.

Minium (see Red Lead)

Mortification is a process during which the substance undergoes a kind of death, usually through a putrefaction, and seems to have been destroyed and its active power lost, but eventually is revived.

Mosaic Gold is golden-yellow glistening scales of crystalline stannic sulfide, made by heating a mixture of tin filings, sulfur and sal ammoniac.

Multiplication is a process of Distillation and Coagulation in which the power of transmutation is concentrated; an increase in the amount of the Stone as obtained from its pristine form. It is represented by the sign for the constellation of Aquarius. Multiplication is the operation by which the powder of projection has its power multiplied.

- N -

Naples Yellow (Cassel yellow) is an oxychloride of lead, made by heating litharge with sal ammoniac.

Natron means salt, though this word usually refers to native sodium carbonate. To the early alchemists, however, the word Natron stood for the basic principle in all salt formation and the creation of bodies in general. The Egyptians accumulated the white salts formed from the evaporation of lakes and used them to preserve mummies. Known as soda ash (sodium carbonate), the oldest deposits are in the Sinai desert. Another naturally-occurring sodium compound mined by the Egyptians was cubic-saltpeter (sodium nitrate). The alchemists referred to both these salts as Natron (from the Arabic word for soda ash), because they suspected that both had a common signature or archetypal basis. Common salt is sodium chloride (NaCl).

Nickel was named by the copper miners of Westphalia the '"kupfer-nickel" or false copper.

Nitrum Flammans is ammonium nitrate made by Glauber.

Nix Alba (see Philosophers' Wool)

- O -

Oil of Vitriol is sulfuric acid made by distilling green vitriol.

Orpiment (Auri-pigmentum). Orpriment is yellow ore of arsenic; arsenic trisulfide.

Ouroboros (Uroboros) is the symbolic rendition of the eternal principles presented in the Emerald Tablet. The great serpent devouring itself represents the idea that "All Is One," even though the universe undergoes periodic cycles of destruction and creation (or resurrection). In Orphic and Mithraic symbology, the Ouroboros was called the *Agathos Daimon* or "Good Spirit" and was a symbol for the "Operation of the Sun." In Greek terminology, the Ouroboros was the *Aion*, which Herakleitos likened to a child at play. To the Greeks, the *Aion* (from which our word "eon" is derived) defined the cosmic period between the creation and destruction of the universe.

- P -

Pearl White is the basic nitrate of bismuth, used by the alchemist Lemery as a cosmetic.

Pelican is a circulatory vessel with two side-arms feeding condensed vapors back into the body. It has a fancied resemblance in shape to a pelican pecking at its breast. Pelicanization is the circulation or rotation of a liquid over a solid performed in the pelican retort.

Philosopher's Stone (see Stone)

Philosophers' Wool or *Nix alba* (white snow) is zinc oxide made by burning zinc in air. Also called Zinc White and used as a pigment.

Potash is potassium carbonate made from the ashes of burnt wood.

Powder of Algaroth is a white powder of antimonious oxychloride, made by precipitation when a solution of butter of antimony in spirit of salt is poured into water.

Precipitation is a process of Coagulation in which solid matter is created during a chemical reaction and falls out of solution. The descent of a substance out of a solution; the precipitate descends to the bottom of the flask.

Preparation is the process by which superfluous substances are removed from the matter and that which is wanting is added to it.

Projection is the final stage of Coagulation in which the power of transformation is directed toward a body; the final process in making gold, in which the Stone or powder Stone (the powder of projection) is tossed upon the molten base metal to transmute it. It is represented by the sign for the constellation of Pisces. The throwing of a ferment or tincture onto a substance in order to effect a transformation of the substance.

Prolectation is the separation of a substance into a subtle and coarser part by the thinning or rarefaction of the subtler parts of the substance, rather than the coarsening of the earthy part.

Pulverization is the breaking down of a substance to smaller fragments through being repeatedly struck with a blunt instrument, such as a hammer, or mallet.

Pulvis Solaris was the chemical arcanum that represented spirit. The "Powder of the Sun" was a mixture of two powders, Black Solaris and Red Solaris. Combining black antimony with sulfur auretum made Black Pulvis Solaris. Black antimony was a common sulfide of antimony, now known as stibnite. The mineral was smelted and ground fine. Pure sulfur auretum, or "golden sulfur," was made by adding sulfuric acid to a dried mixture of sodium carbonate, sulfur, lime, and antimony. The reaction gave off hydrogen sulfide gas, while the sulfur auretum precipitated to the bottom of the container. Red Pulvis Solaris was made by combining sulfur auretum with a compound of mercury known as red mercuric oxide. Egyptian alchemists associated the serpent with the red mercuric oxide and referred to Red Pulvis Solaris as Pulvis Serpentum. Later alchemists became convinced that Red Pulvis Solaris was indeed the powder of projection that would enable them to transform virtually anything into pure gold.

Purgation is purifying of a substance by casting out a gross part of it.

Purple of Cassius was made by Andreas Cassius in 1685 by precipitating a mixture of gold, stannous and stannic chlorides, with alkali. It was used for coloring glass.

Purple Phase (or Iosis) of the Great Work is the third and final stage of transformation. It is marked by the purpling or reddening of the material and occurs during the Coagulation operation.

Putrefaction is the first stage of the Fermentation operation; a digestion in which decomposing essences are reabsorbed. The process was represented by the symbol for the constellation of Leo. The rotting of a substance, often under a prolonged gentle moist heat. Usually the matter becomes black.

Pyrites are the mineral form of iron disulfide that is stable in air. Sometimes pyrite crystals contain traces of real gold.

- Q -

Queen symbolizes woman, lunar consciousness, and Mercury. The Queen is naked during the early stages but regains her royal robes at the end of her transformation. The Queen united with the King is the operation of Conjunction.

Quicklime is calcium oxide or unslacked lime. Calcium oxide is obtained by heating limestone, egg shells, or any material containing Calcium Carbonate, which is one of the seven arcana of alchemy.

Quicksilver (see Mercury)

Quintessence (Quinta Essentia) is the fifth Element with which the alchemists could work. It was the essential presence of something or someone, the living thing itself that animated or gave something its deepest characteristics. The Quintessence partakes of both the Above and the Below, the mental as well as the material. It can be thought of as the ethereal embodiment of the life force that we encounter in dreams and altered states of consciousness. It is the purest individual essence of something that we must unveil and understand in order to transform it.

- R -

Rarefaction is the making of a substance extremely subtle or thin and airy.

Realgar is the red ore of arsenic. Arsenic disulfide.

Rebis (see Hermaphrodite)

Receiver is the flask attached to the outlet of the condenser tube during distillation which contains the distillate or distilled product.

Rectification is the purification of the matter by means of repeated distillations, the distillate being again distilled.

Red Dragon is the pure red oil of lead. The untamed dragon or First Matter.

Red Lead is triplumbic tetroxide. Formed by roasting litharge in air. Red lead is a scarlet crystalline powder.

Red Lion is the red acetate of lead in its crystalline form.

Reiteration is the repetition of a process, particularly applied to circular distillation, in which the distillate is returned to the vessel, and the process continued for many cycles.

Resin of Copper is cuprous chloride. Made by Robert Boyle in 1664 by heating copper with corrosive sublimate.

Resolution occurs when substances that are mixed together become violently separated by being placed into a solution. Thus milk is resolved by vinegar. This process is opposite to Coagulation.

Restinction is when a substance at white heat is brought to perfection by being quenched in an exalting liquid.

Retort is a spherical container (usually glass) with a long neck or spout. It is used to distill or decompose solutions by the action of heat or acids.

Reverberation is an ignition or calcination at a high temperature, in a reverberatory furnace. It also refers to any furnace that roars with a loud sound.

Revivification is the bringing of a mortified matter back to life, or reactivating it.

Rouge Crocus (Colcothar) is a red variety of ferric oxide formed by burning green vitriol in air.

Rubification is the making of the matter in the alchemical process from white to red.

- S -

Sal Ammoniac is ammonium chloride, as identified by Geber.

Sal Volatile is a volatile alkali; ammonium carbonate made from distilling bones, horns, etc.

Salt is the third heavenly substance in alchemy and represents the final manifestation of the perfected Stone. The Emerald Tablet calls it "the Glory of the Whole Universe." For Paracelsus, Salt was like a balsam the body produced to shield itself from decay. It has also been associated with the Ouroboros, the Stone, and the Astral Body. In general, Salt represents the action of thought on matter, be it the One Mind acting on the One Thing of the universe or the alchemist meditating in his inner laboratory. Common salt is sodium chloride.

Segregation is the separation of a composite substance into its parts.

Separation is the third operation in the alchemy of transformation. Symbols of Separation include swords, scythes, arrows, knives, and hatchets. The operation is symbolized by the sign for the constellation of Scorpio. The making of two opposite components separate from each other; often alternated with the Conjunction process.

Serpents. Two serpents represent the opposing masculine and feminine energies of the Work. Three serpents stand for the three higher principles of Sulfur, Mercury, and Salt. Winged serpents represent volatile substances; wingless serpents represent fixed substances. A crucified serpent represents the fixation of the volatile.

Silver is one of the seven metals of alchemy. It is associated with the operation of Distillation.

Skeletons signify the processes of Calcination and Putrefaction, on all the levels in which they occur.

Slaked Lime is calcium hydroxide.

Soda Ash is sodium carbonate formed by burning plants growing on the sea shore.

Solve is to dissolve.

Soul in alchemy is the passive presence in all of us that survives through all eternity and is therefore part of the original substance (First Matter) of the universe. Ultimately, it is the One Thing of the universe. Soul was considered beyond the four material elements and thus conceptualized as a fifth element (or Quintessence).

Soxhlet Extractor is an automatic maceration device made of glass. It is used to extract tinctures from substances using water, alcohol, wine, etc.

Spirit in alchemy is the active presence in all of us that strives toward perfection. Spirit seeks material manifestation for expression. Ultimately, it is the One Mind of the universe.

Spirit of Hartshorn (see Sal Volatile)

Spiritus Fumans is stannic chloride, discovered by Libavius in 1605, through distilling tin with corrosive sublimate.

Square or cube is symbolic of matter and the Four Elements of creation.

Stibnite is antimony trisulfide, the gray mineral ore of antimony.

Stone is the end result of a working. The ultimate Stone is the goal of the Great Work of the whole universe. It was viewed as a magical touchstone that could immediately perfect any substance or situation. The Philosopher's Stone has been associated with the Salt of the World, the Astral Body, the Elixir, and even Jesus Christ.

Stratification is an operation that produces layers in the substance in the flask.

Subduction is the separation of an abstraction downward of the subtle part, as in filtration.

Sublimation is the first stage of Coagulation or last stage of Distillation, in which the vapors solidify; represented by the sign for the constellation of Libra. The vaporization of a solid without fusion or melting, followed by the condensation of its vapor in the resolidified form on a cool surface. The elevation of a dry thing by fire, with adherency to its vessel. This occurs when a solid is heated and gives off a vapor that condenses on the cool upper parts of the vessel as a solid, not going through a liquid phase. An example is sal ammoniac.

Subtilation is the separation of the subtle part of a substance from the gross.

Sugar of Lead is lead acetate, Made by dissolving lead oxide in vinegar.

Sulfur (Sulphur) is one of the three heavenly substances. It represents passion and will and is associated with the operation of Fermentation.

- T -

Thion Hudor solution. Zosimus refers to this solution as the "divine water" or "the bile of the serpent." It is a deep reddish-yellow liquid made by boiling flowers of sulfur with slaked lime.

Three Levels. The key to understanding alchemy is to realize that alchemical thought is extremely dynamic and takes places on three levels at once: the physical, the psychological, and the spiritual. Thus turning lead into gold meant not only physically changing the base metal into the noble metal, but also transforming base habits and emotions into golden thoughts and feelings, as well as transmuting our dark and ignoble souls into the golden light of spirit. By developing this ability to think and work on all three levels of reality at once (becoming "thrice-greatest"), the alchemists created a spiritual technology that applied not only to their laboratories but also to their own personalities and to their relationships with other people -- and with God.

Tin is one of the seven metals of the alchemists. It is associated with the operation of Dissolution and the element Water. Pewter (a mixture of lead and tin) represents a metallic state between the operations of Calcination and Dissolution.

Tin Salt is hydrated stannous chloride.

Transudation occurs if the essence appears to sweat out in drops during a descending distillation.

Trees symbolize the processes of transformation. A tree of moons signifies the Lesser or Lunar Work; a tree of suns signifies the Greater or Solar Work.

Triangle represents the three heavenly principles or substances of Sulfur, Mercury, and Salt.

Trituration is the reduction of a substance to a powder, not necessarily by the use of grinding, but by the application of heat. To grind a solid into a powder; to pulverize with a mortar and pestle. Crush. A process just after Calcination, when the ashes are ground into a fine powder for Dissolution.

Turpeth Mineral is a hydrolyzed form of mercuric sulfate; the yellow crystalline powder described by Basil Valentine.

Tuttia (Tutty) (see Cadmia)

- U -

Uroboros (see Ouroboros)

- V -

Venetian White is a mixture of equal parts of white lead and barium sulfate.

Verdigris is the green substance formed by the atmospheric weathering of copper. This is a complex basic carbonate of copper. In more recent times the term 'verdigris' is more correctly applied to copper acetate, made by the action of vinegar on copper.

Vermillion (see Cinnabar or mercuric sulfide)

Viride Aeris is copper chlate or the green oxide of copper.

Vitrification is the making of a substance into a glass but strong heating and sometimes the addition of lime.

Vitriol was the most important liquid in alchemy. It was the one in which all other reactions took place. Vitriol was distilled from an oily, green substance that formed naturally from the weathering of sulfur-bearing gravel. This Green Vitriol is symbolized by the Green Lion in drawings. After the Green Vitriol (copper sulfate) was collected, it was heated and broken down into iron compounds and sulfuric acid. The acid was separated out by distillation. The first distillation produced a brown liquid that stunk like rotten eggs, but further distillation yielded a nearly odorless, yellow oil called simply Vitriol. The acid readily dissolves human tissue and is severely corrosive to most metals, although it has no effect on gold. White Vitriol is zinc sulfate; Blue Vitriol is copper sulfate.

Vitriolification is the making of a Vitriol. Most often, vitriolification of a metal took place by the direct action of oil of Vitriol, but sometimes by a more indirect route.

- W -

Water is one of the Four Elements of alchemy. Water in the alchemical sense carries the archetypal properties of cleansing and purification. It is associated with the operation of Dissolution and represented by the metal tin.

White Arsenic is an arsenious oxide made from arsenical soot from the roasting ovens, purified by sublimation.

White Lead is basic carbonate of lead. Used as a pigment.

White Phase (Leukosis) is the second stage of the Great Work and takes place during Distillation.

White Vitriol is zinc sulfate or zinc sulfide. Described by Basil Valentine. Made by lixiviating roasted zinc blend (zinc sulfide).

Wind Furnace is any furnace whose fire is aided by a wind tunnel or built-in bellows.

Wine is symbolic of the process of Fermentation and the spiritization of matter.

Winged Lion is the sublimated salt used to make the Philosopher's Stone.

Wismuth (see Bismuth).

Wolf (see antimony)

Wood-ash (see Potash)

- X -

Xanthosis (see Yellow Phase)

- Y -

Yellow Phase (Xanthosis) is an intermediate stage that takes place between the Black and White phases of the Great Work. The term was used by Alexandrian alchemists to describe changes that took place during the Fermentation operation.

- Z -

Zaffre is impure cobalt arsenate, leftover after roasting cobalt ore.

Zodiac. According to the Emerald Tablet ("As Above, so Below"), the archetypal energies of the stars find expression on earth and in mankind. In alchemy, it was essential to consult the zodiac before commencing any of the major operations.

ALCHEMY SYMBOLS & CIPHERS

Air ....
alcohol ....
alum ....
amalgam ....
amalgamation, Conjunction ...
ammonia ....
anneal ....
antimony ....
aqua fortis ....
aqua Regis ....
aqua vitae ....
arsenic ....
ash, soot ....
Autumn ....
beeswax ....
bismuth ....
borax ....
brass ....
brimstone ....
Calcination, Aries ......
chalk ....
cinder ....
cinnabar ....
clay ....
Coagulation, fixation, Gemini ..
cobalt ....
compose ....
Congelation ....

Conjunction, Taurus ...

copper ....

corpuscle ....

crucible ....

creation, Sagittarius ....

crystal ....

day and night ....

decompose ....

digestion, Putrefaction, Leo ..

Dissolution, Cancer .....

dissolve, to ....

distill, to ....

Distillation, Virgo ....

dram ....

Earth ....

eggshells ....

element ....

equal amounts (*Ana*) ...

essence, oil ....

ferment ....

Fermentation, Capricorn ...

filter, Separation ....

Fire ....

fumes ....

furnace, refractory ....

glass ....

glass dropper ....

gold ....

gold foil ....

gold litharge ....

gold, potable	X
gravel	▽
hour	⧖
iron	⚹ ⚸ ↟
iron, Mars	♂
iron filings	⚬⇢
iron oxide, rust	⚲
lapis lazuli	♄
lead, Saturn	♄ ♄ ♄ ♄
lead, red	♆
lime	♒
lye	△
magnesia	⚬⇢ ⅅ ♉
magnet	⟋
manure	☉
mercury, Mercury	☿ ♆ ☿
Multiplication, Aquarius	♒
Neptune, quick lime	♆
nickel	♉ ♀
night	♀
nitric acid	♂
nitre oil	∞
oil	∴ X ♃
ounce	℥
pinch of	P
pint	O
platinum	☽☉
Pluto	♀
powder	₱

potash .... ⛢ ⚸

potassium .... ♃

pound .... ℔

precipitate, the ....

precipitate, to ....

Projection, Pisces ..... ♓

pulverize ....

purify ....

retort, Dissolution, aludel ...

retort, receiver ....

sal ammoniac .... ✳

salt .... ⊕ ☽ ☿

salt, rock .... ♉ ♉

salt, sea ....

saltpeter .... ◐

sediment ....   ♂

Separation, Scorpio ... ♏

silver .... ☽ ♈ ☿

spirit ....

Spring ....

still (distillery) ....

stone ....

Sublimation, Coagulation ... ♌ ♌

sublimate, scales, Libra ... ♎ Ω

sublime, to ....

sugar .... Σ

sulfur ....

sulfuric acid ....

Summer ....

tartar	♏ ♓
tin, Jupiter	♃ ♃ ♓
tin, spirit of	♂̶
Uranus	♅
urine	♀
vitriol	♄
wine	♯°
wine, spirit of	△
vapor bath	♈
vinegar	┼ ♏
vinegar, distilled	✳ ✕
water	▽ ▽
wax	♁
wood	♂
yields	?
Winter	⌂
zinc	♃

TRUE-TYPE FONTS

Meaning	Symbol	Keystroke
1,000	m	7
100	C	6
50	L	8
500	D	9
Air	△	M
alum		[
amalgam		u
amalgamation, Conjunction		p
anneal		m
antimony		\
antimony		b
ash, crucible		k
brass		]
Calcination, Aries	♈	A
Coagulation, fixation, Gemini	Ⅱ	C
cobalt		^
compose		q
congelation		x
Conjunction, Taurus		>
Congelation, Taurus		B
copper		T
copper		_
creation, Sagittarius		I
day, aluminum			
decompose		o

Term		Key
digestion, Putrefaction, Leo	♌	E
Dissolution, Cancer		D
dissolve		r
Distillation, Virgo	♍	F
dram	ʒ	*
Earth	▽	O
equal amounts (*Ana*)	Ā	)
essence, oil	♃	t
ferment, Fermentation		n
Fermentation, Capricorn	♑	J
filter	ƒ	!
Fire	△	N
five	V	4
furnace, refractory	♁	i
gold, Sol	☉	Q
gold		`
hour		{
iron		a
iron, Mars	♂	U
lead, Saturn	♄	W
magnesia		c
mercury, Mercury	☿	S
mercury, spirit of		d
month	⊠	~
Multiplication, Aquarius	♒	K
Neptune, quick lime	♆	Y
nickel		e
night	♀	}
one		1
ounce	ʒ	,
pinch of	P	+

pint		/
platinum		g
Pluto		Z
pound		-
precipitate, the		z
precipitate, to		=
Projection, Pisces		L
retort, Dissolution, aludel		s
retort, receiver		v
salt		;
salt, rock		w
scruple		.
Separation, Scorpio		H
Silver, Luna		R
silver		h
Sublimation, Coagulation		<
Sublimation, scales, Libra		G
take		@
ten		5
three		3
tin		f
tin		j
tin, Jupiter		V
two		2
Uranus		X
wine		#,$
vinegar		y
Water		P
zinc		I

ALCHEMY RESOURCES

BOOKS

Albertus, Frater. *Alchemists Handbook: Manual for Practical Laboratory Alchemy*. Samuel Weiser, 1974. First modern guide to practical alchemy.

Aromatico, Andrea. *Alchemy: The Great Secret*. Harry Abrams, 2000. An illustrated history exploring alchemy's mix of science, philosophy, art, religion, and magic.

Ash, Heather and Noble, Vicki. *The Four Elements of Change*. Council Oak Books, 2004. Using the Four Elements to create a solid foundation to support your mind, body, and spirit.

Bartlett, Robert. *Real Alchemy: A Primer of Practical Alchemy*. Spagyricus, 2007. Explores experimental techniques for beginning the Great Work in the laboratory.

Beyerl, Paul. *Compendium of Herbal Magic*. Phoenix Publishing, 1998. Guide to magical properties of herbs includes planetary associations.

Cavalli, Thom. *Alchemical Psychology*. Tarcher, 2002. Ancient alchemical recipes for living in the modern world.

Cunningham, Scott. *Complete Book of Incense, Oils, and Brews*. Llewellyn Publications, 2002. Guide to preparing essential oils and using them to make incense, balms, and lotions.

Eason, Cassandra. *Alchemy at Work*. Crossing Press, 2004. How to use the ancient arts to enhance your life at work.

Edinger, Edward. *Anatomy of the Psyche: Alchemical Symbolism in Psychotherapy*. Open Court Publishing, 1991. In-depth description of the operations of alchemy in psychological terms.

Goddard, David. *Tower of Alchemy*. Samuel Weiser, 1999. Filled with Hermetic principles that are meant to be applied and the spiritual level.

Green, Mindy and Keville, Kathi. *Aromatherapy: A Complete Guide to the Healing Art.* Crossing Press, 1995. Shows how to use, blend, and prepare essential oils at home.

Hauck, Dennis William. *Complete Idiot's Guide to Alchemy.* Penguin Alpha, 2008. The complete guide to all aspects of alchemy, including the practical, psychological, and spiritual work.

Hauck, Dennis William. *The Emerald Tablet: Alchemy for Personal Transformation.* Penguin Arkana, 1999. Definitive history of the Emerald Tablet and the application of its principles to personal transformation.

Hauck, Dennis William. *Sorcerer's Stone: A Beginner's Guide to Alchemy.* Athanor Press, 2013. Makes alchemy come alive with clear explanations, fascinating anecdotes, and hands-on experiments.

Junius, Manfred. *Spagyrics: Alchemical Preparation of Medicinal Essences, Tinctures, and Elixirs.* Healing Arts Press, 2007. Classic guide to the art of extracting plant essences includes elixir recipes from famous alchemists.

Linden, Stanton. *The Alchemy Reader: From Hermes Trismegistus to Isaac Newton.* Cambridge University, 2003. Basic writings of the alchemists ranging from Alexandria to the end of the seventeenth century.

Marlan, Stanton. *Black Sun: Alchemy and Art of Darkness.* Texas A&M Press, 2005. Examines the alchemical stage of Nigredo, the blackening or mortification from which the true light emerges.

Martin, Sean. *Alchemy and Alchemists.* Chartwell Books, 2007. Basic review of the history and methods of alchemy.

Melville, Francis. *Book of Alchemy.* Barron's, 2002. Presents the seven operations of the Emerald Tablet, as well as an illustrated overview of alchemy.

Miller, Richard, and Iona Miller. *Modern Alchemist.* Phanes Press, 1994. Guide to personal transformation using the principles of alchemy.

Moring, Gary. *Complete Idiot's Guide to Understanding Einstein.* Alpha, 2004. Great introduction to modern physics that contains an interesting section on alchemy.

Moring, Gary. *Complete Idiot's Guide to Theories of the Universe.* Alpha, 2001. Guide to modern cosmology and quantum physics that lays the foundation for the ideas of modern alchemy.

Reich, Wilhelm. *Secret of the Golden Flower.* Harcourt Brace, 1988. Taoist alchemy treatise with wonderful commentary by Carl Jung.

Rolfe, Randy. *The Four Temperaments.* Marlowe & Company, 2002. Understanding the Elements as alchemical humors that allow you to fine tune your health, career, and relationships.

Roob, Alexander. *Alchemy & Mysticism.* Taschen, 1997. Stunning pictorial presentation of the spiritual practice of alchemy.

Stavish, Mark. *Path of Alchemy: Energetic Healing and the World of Natural Magic.* Llewellyn, 2006. Guide to the teachings of Hermes and their applications in alchemy and healing.

Von Franz, Marie-Louise. *Alchemy: An Introduction to the Symbolism and the Psychology.* Inner City Books, 1980. Inspiring guide to spiritual wholeness that follows the Jungian interpretation.

Whitmont, Edward. *Alchemy of Healing: Psyche and Soma.* North Atlantic Books, 1996. Challenges the methods of mechanical medicine and emphasizes the importance of consciousness in healing.

Wolf, Fred Alan. *The Spiritual Universe.* Moment Point Press, 1998. Presents one physicist's vision of spirit, soul, matter, and self in the universe.

Wolf. Fred Alan. *Matter Into Feeling: A New Alchemy of Science and Spirit.* Moment Point Press, 2002. Examines the science behind consciousness, memory, dreams, and the "One-Mind" concept of the alchemists.

Wolf, Fred Alan. Mind *into Matter: A New Alchemy of Science and Spirit.* Moment Point Press, 2000. Interprets modern physics in terms of ancient spiritual texts from alchemy, the Qabala, and the Eastern traditions.

Yudelove, Eric. *Tao and the Tree of Life: Alchemical and Sexual Mysteries of the East and West.* Llewellyn, 1996. Decodes the mysteries of the Tao and Kabbalah to show their underlying basis in alchemy.

INTERNET RESOURCES

Alchemergy is devoted to modern alchemy films and filmmaking as it applies to personal, social, and global transformation. Facebook: www.facebook.com/groups/alchemergy/, Web: www.Alchemergy.net

Alchemy Conferences has lecture videos from conferences held by the International Alchemy Guild. Web: www.AlchemyConference.net.

Alchemy Guild is the official website of the International Alchemy Guild (IAG) with over 500 members around the world. Facebook: www.facebook.com/groups/2220753444/. Web: www.AlchemyGuild.org

Alchemy Museum in San Jose, California, features historic artifacts and books about Western alchemy. Web: www.AlchemyMuseum.info. Facebook: www.facebook.com/groups/alchemymuseum/.

Alchemy of Consciousness is Dennis William Hauck's alchemy resource web. YouTube channel: www.YouTube.com/user/alchemergist. Web: www.DWHauck.com.

Alchemy Study Program features certification courses in both practical and spiritual alchemy. www.AlchemyStudy.com | www.AlchemyStudy.org Faceboook: www.facebook.com/groups/studyalchemy/ and www.facebook.com/groups/alchemical.elixirs/.

Alchemy Web Site is Adam McLean's huge resource of original texts, drawings, and articles on practical and spiritual alchemy. Web: http://levity.com/alchemy

Crucible.org is a central supply source for alchemists with links to lab supplies, glassware, chemicals, herbs, oils, tinctures, books, artwork, jewelry, and other Hermetic items. Web: www.Crucible.org

Kymia Arts is Avery Hopkins' site devoted to bridging the gap between practical and spiritual sides of alchemy. Web: www.KymiaArts.com.

Paracelsus College in Australia was founded in 1984 by Frater Albertus and offers resources in practical and spiritual alchemy. http://homepages.ihug.com.au/~panopus/

Spagyria is John Reid's website on practical plant alchemy and the art of spagyrics. Web: www.spagyria.com

Spagyricus is Robert Bartlett's website on practical alchemy and applications in spagyrics. Web: www.Spagyricus.com.

www.ingramcontent.com/pod-product-compliance
Lightning Source LLC
Chambersburg PA
CBHW060704280326
41933CB00012B/2296